CIHM
Microfiche
Series
(Monographs)

ICMH
Collection de
microfiches
(monographies)

Canadian Institute for Historical Microreproductions / Institut canadien de microreproductions historiques

© 1999

Technical and Bibliographic Notes / Notes techniques et bibliographiques

The Institute has attempted to obtain the best original copy available for filming. Features of this copy which may be bibliographically unique, which may alter any of the images in the reproduction, or which may significantly change the usual method of filming are checked below.

L'Institut a microfilmé le meilleur exemplaire qu'il lui a été possible de se procurer. Les détails de cet exemplaire qui sont peut-être uniques du point de vue bibliographique, qui peuvent modifier une image reproduite, ou qui peuvent exiger une modification dans la méthode normale de filmage sont indiqués ci-dessous.

- [✓] Coloured covers / Couverture de couleur
- [ ] Covers damaged / Couverture endommagée
- [ ] Covers restored and/or laminated / Couverture restaurée et/ou pelliculée
- [ ] Cover title missing / Le titre de couverture manque
- [ ] Coloured maps / Cartes géographiques en couleur
- [ ] Coloured ink (i.e. other than blue or black) / Encre de couleur (i.e. autre que bleue ou noire)
- [ ] Coloured plates and/or illustrations / Planches et/ou illustrations en couleur
- [ ] Bound with other material / Relié avec d'autres documents
- [ ] Only edition available / Seule édition disponible
- [ ] Tight binding may cause shadows or distortion along interior margin / La reliure serrée peut causer de l'ombre ou de la distorsion le long de la marge intérieure.
- [ ] Blank leaves added during restorations may appear within the text. Whenever possible, these have been omitted from filming / Il se peut que certaines pages blanches ajoutées lors d'une restauration apparaissent dans le texte, mais, lorsque cela était possible, ces pages n'ont pas été filmées.
- [✓] Additional comments / Commentaires supplémentaires: Various pagings.

- [ ] Coloured pages / Pages de couleur
- [ ] Pages damaged / Pages endommagées
- [ ] Pages restored and/or laminated / Pages restaurées et/ou pelliculées
- [✓] Pages discoloured, stained or foxed / Pages décolorées, tachetées ou piquées
- [✓] Pages detached / Pages détachées
- [✓] Showthrough / Transparence
- [ ] Quality of print varies / Qualité inégale de l'impression
- [ ] Includes supplementary material / Comprend du matériel supplémentaire
- [ ] Pages wholly or partially obscured by errata slips, tissues, etc., have been refilmed to ensure the best possible image / Les pages totalement ou partiellement obscurcies par un feuillet d'errata, une pelure, etc., ont été filmées à nouveau de façon à obtenir la meilleure image possible.
- [ ] Opposing pages with varying colouration or discolourations are filmed twice to ensure the best possible image / Les pages s'opposant ayant des colorations variables ou des décolorations sont filmées deux fois afin d'obtenir la meilleure image possible.

This item is filmed at the reduction ratio checked below / Ce document est filmé au taux de réduction indiqué ci-dessous.

10x		14x		18x		22x		26x		30x	
	12x		16x		20x		24x		28x		32x

The copy filmed here has been reproduced thanks to the generosity of:

National Library of Canada

The images appearing here are the best quality possible considering the condition and legibility of the original copy and in keeping with the filming contract specifications.

Original copies in printed paper covers are filmed beginning with the front cover and ending on the last page with a printed or illustrated impression, or the back cover when appropriate. All other original copies are filmed beginning on the first page with a printed or illustrated impression, and ending on the last page with a printed or illustrated impression.

The last recorded frame on each microfiche shall contain the symbol → (meaning "CONTINUED"), or the symbol ▽ (meaning "END"), whichever applies.

Maps, plates, charts, etc., may be filmed at different reduction ratios. Those too large to be entirely included in one exposure are filmed beginning in the upper left hand corner, left to right and top to bottom, as many frames as required. The following diagrams illustrate the method:

L'exemplaire filmé fut reproduit grâce à la générosité de:

Bibliothèque nationale du Canada

Les images suivantes ont été reproduites avec le plus grand soin, compte tenu de la condition et de la netteté de l'exemplaire filmé, et en conformité avec les conditions du contrat de filmage.

Les exemplaires originaux dont la couverture en papier est imprimée sont filmés en commençant par le premier plat et en terminant soit par la dernière page qui comporte une empreinte d'impression ou d'illustration, soit par le second plat, selon le cas. Tous les autres exemplaires originaux sont filmés en commençant par la première page qui comporte une empreinte d'impression ou d'illustration et en terminant par la dernière page qui comporte une telle empreinte.

Un des symboles suivants apparaîtra sur la dernière image de chaque microfiche, selon le cas: le symbole → signifie "A SUIVRE", le symbole ▽ signifie "FIN".

Les cartes, planches, tableaux, etc., peuvent être filmés à des taux de réduction différents. Lorsque le document est trop grand pour être reproduit en un seul cliché, il est filmé à partir de l'angle supérieur gauche, de gauche à droite, et de haut en bas, en prenant le nombre d'images nécessaire. Les diagrammes suivants illustrent la méthode.

1	2	3

1
2
3

1	2	3
4	5	6

MICROCOPY RESOLUTION TEST CHART

(ANSI and ISO TEST CHART No. 2)

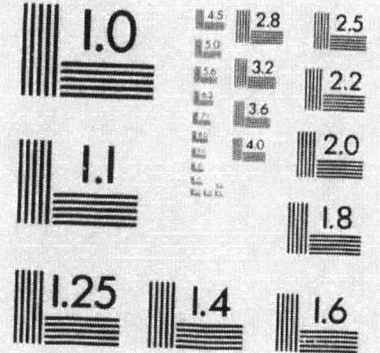

1853 East Main Street
Rochester, New York   14609   USA
(716) 482 – 0300 – Phone
(716) 288 – 5989 – Fax

LETTER TO

REV. A. B. SIMPSON,

PRESIDENT OF THE CHRISTIAN AND MISSIONARY
ALLIANCE, NEW YORK.

REPLYING TO HIS STRICTURES ON THE "PROMOTION" OF COMPANIES.

BY W. J. FENTON.

NATIONAL LIBRARY
CANADA
BIBLIOTHÈQUE NATIONALE

LETTER TO
REV. A. B. SIMPSON,

PRESIDENT OF THE CHRISTIAN AND MISSIONARY
ALLIANCE, NEW YORK.

REPLYING TO HIS STRICTURES ON THE "PROMOTION" OF COMPANIES.

BY W. J. FENTON.

TORONTO, ONT., MARCH, 1902.

BR115
C3
F45
1902

LETTER TO REV. A. B. SIMPSON.

TORONTO, March 15, 1902.

REV. A. B. SIMPSON,
    692 Eighth Avenue,
      New York, U.S.A.

Dear Sir,—" In the world ye shall have tribulation, but in me 'peace,'" is a legacy left by our blessed Lord to His disciples, the reality of which has been abundantly verified in my experience. And the most trying part of this experience has been that the greatest tribulation has come, not from the people of the world, from whom it might naturally have been expected, but from Christians, real or professed, who cannot brook the independence of anyone who might appear to question the soundness of their teaching, or the reality of their professed experience of sinless perfection.

I write you at the present time in consequence of an editorial paragraph in the "Christian and Missionary Alliance," of 8th February, 1902, written immediately after your return from the Alliance Convention in Toronto (which I did not attend), under the heading of "The Spirit of Speculation," which reads as follows:—

"The desire to 'get rich quick' seems to always
" accompany a time of national prosperity, and once
" more is turning the heads of our American people,
" and tempting many into reckless and foolish specu-
" lations in the name of investments. It is really the
" surest way to get poor quick. There is no known
" method of making one dollar worth ten, in arithme-

"tic, ethics, morals, earth, or heaven. It may be
"done in one other place, but it is safer not to go too
"near there. Those who play with these things must
"not wonder if 'the get rich quick' plan turns the
"other side up soon, and becomes the surest path to
"poverty and ruin. The only reasonable and honest
"way to seek for prosperity is by honorable labor
"and legitimate business. Let us advise our friends
"to keep out of all these alluring schemes, that seek
"their hard earnings through shrewd promoters
"and flashy advertisements, whether in the secular
"or religious press."

Under ordinary circumstances, the general tenor of this paragraph could not be objected to, and it would be regarded by the general public as wholesome advice by a public journalist, respecting a crying evil at the present day in the form of dishonest promotion of various trusts. But if it was written at that particular time to wound or injure a Christian known to you, who would have been thankful to have you ask him in an honest and straightforward manner for any explanation, no language can be too strong in which to condemn the exhibition of such a spirit, under the pretext of seeking to promote the public welfare.

About the time when you as a young man had the pastoral oversight of Knox Church in Hamilton, I was preaching the Gospel almost daily in the streets of that city. You were then recognized as possessing great natural gifts, whilst I, without any special endowments for public service, simply tried in dependence upon the guidance of the Holy Spirit to lift up Christ as the Saviour of sinners. And I believe that God, who uses weak things for His own glory, blessed my labors to the salvation of some souls. I was then in the prime of life, in a good financial position, and cheerfully gave up my time and means to the Master's service in the open air, before the advent of the Salvation Army. And at the same time you drew large audiences to listen to your eloquent sermons in Knox Church. But you knew the decided stand that I had then taken as a Christian man.

You removed to Louisville. You met with D. L. Moody, George Muller, and other godly men, and a great change came over your spiritual life. Your remarkable experience of bodily healing led to your unfolding, in a more public and powerful manner than it had been taught before, the truth of Scripture on the subject of Divine Healing. You resigned your position as a Presbyterian minister to engage in independent evangelistic work, in which your labors have been much blessed, but in which you have also attained dangerous prominence through the brilliant talents with which you have been endowed, and you need much grace to keep you humble, and hinder the development of an arbitrary spirit towards those who do not implicitly submit to your wishes in some things.

Your preaching was a means of blessing to my son (then in New York, and now in Heaven), when he was in a backsliding condition, and for this I shall never cease to be grateful. And afterwards, when in a time of great affliction, without human intervention, the Holy Spirit brought before me the Scripture in James V. respecting the anointing for healing, it was through your aid that I was led to more fully understand and act upon that truth, which has ever since been precious to me. And for this aid, and the spiritual blessing connected with it, I have always been deeply grateful.

At the Old Orchard Convention, when the "Christian Alliance" was formed, you placed me on the first organization committee as Vice-President for Canada. I objected to being placed on that committee, and urged you to appoint Rev. John Salmon instead. You insisted, however, and I gave way, after telling you that I did not want to take any prominent position, and that he had been holding some meetings on the subject of Divine Healing in Toronto. After consenting to act, I felt it to be my duty to further the interests of the organization to the best of my ability. How that was done you know. The leading teachers amongst the Brethren, with whom I was then associated, were opposed to my speaking on the subject of Divine Healing in their meetings. I withdrew from their fellowship, and commenced with Mr. Salmon a meeting for worship and the breaking of bread on Lord's Day mornings. This went on prosperously until some women came in, who both held and taught extreme non-eternity views. I objected to their reception. This annoyed Mr. Salmon, and led him finally to withdraw and start another meeting.

Afterwards I arranged for the first Christian Alliance Convention at Hamilton, and assisted to organize the first branch of the Alliance there. And after my return to Toronto, I called together many who were in sympathy with the truth of Divine Healing, and during Mr. Salmon's absence from the city, organized a branch of the Alliance here also, and in order to soothe his ruffled feelings after our separation on the non-eternity question, got him elected as President, whilst I was elected Secretary.

Mr. Salmon and I both took a leading part in the meetings, which were good and largely attended, until after extravagant and unscriptural teaching on the subject of sinless perfection was introduced, when I endeavored to show that such teaching was contrary to the Word of God.

Whilst the meetings were going on prosperously I made arrangements for sending the first four young ladies to the Missionary Training College at New York, who went there from Toronto.

But you made a great mistake in complimenting me too highly, both at the Convention in New York and in the Alliance paper, for my work on behalf of the organization in Canada. I did not need any flattery to urge me to greater energy in a cause wherein my sympathies were already enlisted, and your injudicious remarks in my favor excited the jealousy of those whose unscriptural teaching I had been opposing, who boasted of their experience of sinless perfection, and declared that the only reason why I did not see with them was because I had never had their experience.

When our meetings were going on most prosperously, Mr. Salmon and Dr. Zimmerman announced and began separate meetings, not far distant from our Alliance meeting, and at the same hour, with a view to establishing a new church organization. About the same time the woman to whom I was afterwards married, informed me that Mr. Salmon had told her that the opening of their new meeting would be the means of "rooting Fenton out of Toronto," and she declared she was so much shocked at his talking in that way that she had to tell me about it. Is it any wonder that I should feel distressed on hearing of such a statement having been made by one who professed to be a fellow-laborer in the Lord's work, and that I should be thoroughly disgusted with the kind of holiness teaching that could lead to such a development? After my marriage I told him what I had heard, without giving the name of my informant, and he positively denied having ever made such a statement. My wife, however, had professed to receive healing of serious heart trouble and great spiritual blessing through my instrumentality, and I believed her word in preference to his, because of the spirit he had manifested on several occasions. She continued to attend the Alliance meetings with me after he had separated, both before and after our marriage, and I never suspected her of having told a deliberate falsehood, and her extreme kindness towards me even during the life of her former husband, and her professed sympathy with my views of scriptural truth, led me to think that I would find in her a worthy help-meet in future spiritual service. In this, however, I was woefully mistaken, but her true character did not become fully manifest until I had lost all my properties, and the utter lack of any true affection was sorely felt in my time of need.

Both meetings were continued for some time with about equal numbers attending each, and at length the leaders in Mr. Salmon's meeting invited Mr. Dowie to come to Toronto for the purpose of holding meetings. They joined his "Divine Healing Association" here, in which your teaching on that subject was publicly attacked, and got most of those attending the Alliance meetings to join it with them.

I continued to carry on the Alliance meetings until your next Convention in Toronto, for which I made all arrangements as formerly, but with much greater difficulty, because of the want of proper co-operation. You knew what had been going on, but took no action to aid in setting matters right, and finding that the Alliance meeting that I was trying to keep together was only regarded as one in opposition to Mr. Dowie's Divine Healing Association, and the extreme holiness people, I gave it up and withdrew from the Alliance altogether, for the sake of peace.

At your next Convention in Toronto I attended your meetings, and at the close of one of them I went up to the platform and greeted you cordially, but you received me with great coldness. I saw that you were displeased with me about something, and could not imagine what it was, except that I had withdrawn from the Alliance under the circumstances stated, and, after a final attempt had been made by some one to teach me some holiness theories by means of an abusive anonymous letter. As I was anxious to know if there was anything else in which I might have given you offence, I wrote you very fully, giving particulars of the circumstances that led to my withdrawal, and expressing my willingness to answer any questions you might put in reference to anything you had heard against me that might appear to justify the manner in which you had acted towards me. I believe that this was the honest, straightforward course to take, and supposed that you would meet me in the same spirit as an honest Christian man. But you never answered my letter or even acknowledged its receipt.

For many years I have been silently, if not always patiently, suffering from defamation by brethren who would not dare to charge me openly with wrongdoing as a Christian business man, and it appears to me that now, in the evening of my earthly life, it is high time once for all to put a stop to the wicked slanders that have been circulated against me.

When the paragraph referred to was written, you had just left Toronto, where my wife is in fellowship with the Bethany meeting, and on intimate terms with Mr. and Mrs. Salmon and others connected with the Alliance work, and where it is well known that I am engaged in "promoting" the establishment of a legitimate and necessary business. These facts, coupled with the unreasonable ill-feeling shown towards me by some of the extreme Holiness people, whose teaching I could not endorse, have led me naturally to think that your editorial notice may have been inspired by what you heard about me from these parties in Toronto.

If you can honestly say, as in the presence of God, that there was in your mind, when writing that paragraph, no reference to me, I shall endeavor to give you full credit for the repudiation of any improper motives. But if you cannot do this, I must regard you as guilty of making an unjustifiable attack upon one who had frankly invited you to question him about any slanders you might have heard against him. It will be no excuse to say that the paragraph was only a general statement applicable to many persons, if your own conscience convicts you of having listened to slander without asking what I had to say about it. And if you sat down and deliberately framed that paragraph, so as to identify me with it in the estimation of those in this city who take your paper, and at the same time to impute to me falsely, either improper motives, or dishonorable conduct, in any way, I must tell you plainly that your action in this case is entirely at variance with the advice given by you to others on the next page of the same issue of your paper, as follows:—" You will never be sorry for putting the best possible construction upon the doings of others."

If in this matter you have willfully tried to do me an injury, I have no doubt that, when all the facts in this connection become known, you will be sorry that you did not act upon this good advice yourself.

I have thought of you more highly, perhaps, than I ought to think of any poor fallible mortal, and have often stood up in your defence when others charged you with wrong-doing, and you are the last man in the world who should have made an attack which appears to be both cruel and vindictive, if that paragraph was intended to aply to me, as it will certainly be understood by others in this city.

It is not wrong to promote the establishment of a legitimate and necessary business, so long as the promotion of it is honestly conducted, and so long as the motive in such promotion is not to acquire wealth for selfish gratification or worldly ambition. To assert the contrary is simply to talk nonsense. The right or wrong of a Christian being in any business which is in itself lawful, depends entirely upon the motive that prompts him to engage in it.

As you have insinuated that those engaged in the promotion of companies must necessarily be actuated by sordid or dishonest motives, and have not asked me for any explanation, I take the liberty of giving you a brief statement regarding my financial affairs, and the circumstances which led to the " promotion " of a company by me, and at the same time to the separation from my wife, on 20th March, 1900, who is now connected with your Alliance meeting in this city.

Over thirty years ago I purchased at very low

prices over 6,000 acres of wild lands, on many of which balances were due to the Government, to pay which I borrowed money and gave mortgages as security. Until the opening up of Manitoba these lands were rapidly increasing in value, with ready sales, so that I seemed to have acquired a competency, and for several years I devoted my time and means chiefly to the Lord's service, and aiding others who were so engaged. But after the boom in Manitoba lands took place, the timbered lands owned by me in Ontario became unsalable, and I was so burdened with interest on mortgages and taxes, that it was a constant struggle to meet my engagements. This led me to engage in real estate business, chiefly with a view to getting honorably freed from all liabilities to others, and again engaging in Gospel service, that had more attraction for me than any other business. After some years of very severe trial, through family affliction and disappointments in business, my labors appeared to be crowned with so much success that I counted upon speedily disposing of all my properties, getting freed from all liabilities to others, and thus being free to spend the rest of my life in the Lord's service.

About this time, after having been about seven years a widower, I married the widow of a humble carpenter, who, as it afterwards became apparent, supposed I was wealthy because I was possessed of so much property.

Shortly afterwards the terrible re-action in real estate values set in, by means of which many hundreds of persons were ruined who had been supposed wealthy. Most of my properties had been purchased subject to mortgages. Rents as well as values suddenly went down to such an extent that I found it impossible to meet my engagements, and I assigned all my properties for the benefit of my creditors. As city properties became unsalable, the commission business, which was my only means of support, yielded very little revenue. Before the final crisis came, however, and whilst I supposed that the depression in values was only temporary, I was much troubled with heart failure, and, fearing that my wife might be left in want, I placed a policy of insurance upon my life for $4,000 as a provision for her support in event of my being taken away suddenly. This was done without her knowledge, and without prayerful consideration, and the results of this wrong step were most unhappy. From this time forward the keeping up of that policy was with her the most important consideration, and a remarkable change took place in her deportment towards me. Home duties were neglected, and most disagreeable conduct indulged in, except when strangers were present, and then her face would be wreathed in smiles, and her manners fascinating.

As times grew worse I was unable to pay the premiums on the policy as they became due, without borrowing the money from her married daughter at ten per cent. interest, and then got no peace from either of them until it was repaid, although the daughter had nearly $2,000 of bank deposits lying at her credit. After much opposition from them, I at length got the amount of policy reduced to $2,000, on which, at my time of life, the premiums were still very heavy for one in my circumstances. When it became fully evident that all my properties had been hopelessly lost, and that for a long time very little would be earned by selling for other people on commission, and having been often reduced to my last cent, I came to the conclusion that it would not be right to borrow any more money to pay premiums. This led to such a time of persecution by both mother and daughter as almost worried me to death. They knew that the policy would lapse in a few weeks if the premium was not paid, and they could not bear the thought of missing the chance of getting the amount of my insurance, which seemed almost within their grasp. During this time of dark trial, when the struggle was going on about the cancellation of my policy, I had often to complain of not getting sufficient nourishment, and was constantly troubled with heart failure, and it seemed as if at any time I might pass away. God alone knew how I was tormented by those two women. At length I got my nephew, who is a doctor, to examine my heart, and he said that mental worry was the main cause of trouble. I then confided to him for the first time, what I had hitherto kept to myself, the way in which I had been treated since placing the policy on my life, and more especially since I had decided to allow it to lapse. He advised me not to renew it on any consideration, and in the meantime to go away somewhere for a change. This, however, I could not afford to do, and as the next best alternative he advised me to rent a room in a private boarding house, to which I could walk after tea, get a quiet night's rest, and then walk back home before breakfast in the morning. He also advised me to go to a restaurant occasionally and get some nourishing food, so as to keep up my strength. This advice was acted upon, the strife of tongues was avoided during the night, quiet sleep was secured, and the condition of my heart was much improved. After the time for the renewal of the policy had passed, I gave up the room in which I had been lodging for several weeks, and no one but the doctor knew why I had rented it, as the only reason given to others was that the doctor had recommended the walk after tea and before breakfast for some trouble that I had with my heart.

It was during this time of domestic misery that I wrote two books that were afterwards published. "The Unity of the Spirit; or the Failure of Brethrenism as a United Testimony," and "The Riddle of Existence Solved," as a reply to Professor Goldwin Smith's "Guesses at the Riddle of Existence." No business was being done in my office, and after commencing to recover strength through following the doctor's advice, and God's blessing upon the means thus used, I did not wish to be idle, and asked the Lord to enable me to use my pen for His glory, and for blessing to others, and although I had very little experience in that kind of work, I believe that He did guide me in it, and that some souls have been profited by it.

Just after the writing of the second and larger of these books had been finished, I got employment in the placing of the stock of a new Trusts Company by personal canvass, which is now doing business here. In this work I was prospered, so as to be enabled within about two years not only to pay for the publishing of my two books, but also to pay off a good many small debts which had been contracted before my assignment was made, and which I regarded myself as in honor bound to pay afterwards. After getting through with the sale of their stock I was engaged by the Trusts Company as their Inspector.

I had for some time been making it a subject of prayer that the Lord would open up the way whereby I could earn sufficient means to get freed from all liabilities to others whilst still in the body, and that, if it pleased Him to provide more, I might be enabled to use it in His service, and for His glory.

Shortly afterwards my attention was directed to the change just commencing from Wood to Wire in the whole farm and railway fencing of the country. I collected information and statistics on the subject, and submitted them to a number of gentlemen, all of whom admitted the necessity for the manufacture and introduction of some superior styles of Wire Fencing, for which there must shortly be a great demand. A charter was obtained from the Provincial Government, and a Company organized for the purpose of meeting this demand, and I firmly believe that God has in answer to prayer, wonderfully guided in all its affairs, not always as we desired, but as He saw best. As the establishment of this business on such a basis as to pay fair dividends must be gradual, an arrangement was made with a Trusts Company, securing to the holders of the Preferred Stock, which we are selling, a fair rate of interest for the first five years, whilst power looms are being built, and other preliminary work is being done. And it is clearly understood that no dividend shall be declared until it has been fairly earned by the product of the machines that we are building. This arrangement is very satisfactory to our own shareholders, who receive their interest regularly every half year, but it excited much hostility amongst other Companies and Brokers having stocks for sale, and we have also had a good deal of opposition from other parties engaged in the same line of business, so that the sale of our stock has been much slower than we hoped and expected. This, however, has been over-ruled for good, because we have only to pay interest upon the amount of capital that is actually paid up while preliminary work is being done. But it gives me much pleasure to inform you that our work is going on steadily and economically, that all our obligations have been promptly met, and that we have a considerable balance of cash on hand, without using in the business one-half of our paid-up capital. That I have the confidence of those whose means are invested in the business is shown by the fact that when the Report and Financial Statements submitted to the shareholders in January last, at our Annual Meeting, were unanimously approved, all the Directors, including myself, were re-elected.

When the organization of this Company was decided upon, I told my wife about it, and the objects that I had in view if my labors prospered, and I also told her that the office of the new Company might be that in our own house which I had used in the real estate business, and that it would be necessary for me to have a stenographer and typewriter, as I would have much correspondence, and must be away from home a great deal while placing the stock. She at once asked if I intended to have "a girl typewriter," and I said "Yes," and she answered, "Why can't you have a young man?" I told her that a young woman would suit me much better, as I would have to be so much away from home, and a young woman would be company for her in my absence. She had made up her mind, however, that no young woman should be engaged, and I was as fully decided that in this case I would not submit to her dictation, as I had often done before for the sake of peace. The next morning, as we sat down to breakfast, she said that she had a proposition to make, namely, that I should give her a separation, allow her $20 per month for support, and purchase some of the furniture which belonged to her. I told her at once that I would not consent to any such proposal, and asked her what would anyone think if told that two persons, who both professed to be Christians, could not live in the same house together. To eat breakfast that morning was, of course, out of the question, and she went on at such a rate that I was obliged for the sake of peace for some time afterwards to take all my meals at a restaurant. There was a lull in the storm for some time whilst delay occurred in the organization of the Company, but on my return home one night from the President's office, I told her that he had shown me a letter from a young lady attending college, who was a friend of his family, reminding him of his promise to be on the look-out for a position for her, that I had advised him to offer her the situation in our office, which it had then been decided was to be down town, instead of at our house, as at first proposed, and that he had promised to do so. This caused a fresh outburst of ill-temper and scolding, which lasted intermittently for, I think, about two weeks, until the evening on which agreements regarding the new company were finally settled. That evening, whilst in my office busily engaged in preparing some matter to be put in the printer's hands the next morning, my wife came down from her room and got at me again about a separation, but I positively declined even to speak on the subject, as I had so much work to do before retiring to rest. After persisting for some time in vain, she at length returned to her room. When I had finished my work I was so worn out that my head had not long touched the pillow before I was sound asleep. The next morning, on waking, the wretched experience of the past few weeks came before my mind, and something seemed to say to me, "Let her have her own way." I had then some money in hand, and expected soon to earn more. Regarding the suggestion as coming from God for my deliverance from an intolerable burden that was wearing my life out, I went at once to her room and told her that, as she still persisted in her demand after my positive refusal, I had decided to let her have her own way about a separation. She asked, "When ?" and I said that if she wished it I would at once instruct my solicitor to prepare the necessary agreement. To this she assented, the agreement was drawn up the same day, and executed in the evening. That night she worked till a very late hour, packing up everything she chose to take, without any interference by me. The next morning, whilst I went out to eat some breakfast at a restaurant, she resumed the same work, and continued at it till about noon. In the meantime, after getting something to eat, I had gone to a typewriting office and attempted to dictate some documents, but felt very ill, and this was remarked by those in the office, who urged me to go home and lie down. I took their advice, and made my way home with great difficulty. When I went in I told my wife that my heart was troubling me so much that I could not work longer, and must lie down for a rest before trying to do more. Without a word in reply, she turned her back on me and resumed her packing, whilst I slowly climbed the stairs to my room and lay down on the bed. When her waggon was loaded with all she chose to take, she came to my room and said "Good bye."

I did not see her again till the following Saturday, when she called and asked me for a gold watch which I had presented to her years before, and which she had left in a drawer. On receiving this she at once took her departure.

If I were to repeat this woman's language, or describe her conduct on many occasions, I think you would agree with me that I have abundant reason to be thankful for a legal separation from her without any public scandal. There is a much darker side of the case, which may yet have to come into the full light of day, but for the sake of her grand-daughters, whom I have known from early childhood, I have refrained from saying more than appeared necessary to show you the unreliability of the source from which the evil speaking about me in your Alliance meeting here has proceeded. For over three years after the wicked conduct of herself and her daughter to which I have only faintly referred, no one but the doctor and my solicitor knew from me how I had been treated. But I am fully aware that, both before and after our final separation, a constant course of defamation has been pursued, and become manifest in the altered demeanor of parties with whom I have been acquainted. It will hardly be credited that, while this woman was acting in the worst possible manner to me at home, she was visiting and carrying fruit to sick men in the Toronto Hospital, and attending mothers' meetings, for the instruction of poor women, and by some of these, doubtless, regarded as an angel of mercy.

It is only a few weeks ago that she told one person that she knew as a fact that I had thousands of dollars by me. This was a deliberate falsehood, told probably for the purpose of justifying her living the idle life she is pursuing at my expense. And at the same time Mrs. Salmon has been telling her friends what a hard time of it poor Mrs. Fenton had when living with me!

I am now thankful that at the time of my enforced idleness in the way of business, and of my torture by both mother and daughter about the insurance policy, I wrote an autobiography of my life since 1st December, 1880, with a diary of my experiences of their conduct. This was written because of conversations which I had overheard between the mother and daughter, in which the latter advised her mother to starve me out, and in which they spoke of saying certain things about me, and said that if I denied they would have the oaths of three against one. This was afterwards handed by me to the doctor, with a letter, of which the following is a copy, to be opened and acted upon in the event of my death, as a means of refuting any slanders affecting my character as a Christian which these women might circulate about me, but at the date of this letter I had not yet spoken to the doctor or any one else about the treatment I had received:—

Toronto, 20th January, 1897.

My Dear Fred,

My wife and her daughter seem determined, if possible, to worry me to death before 15th February. when the next premium on my $2,000 policy in Equitable becomes due, as they know that I do not intend to renew, even if I had the money, which I have not got.

They are well aware of the effect which this worry of mind has upon me, causing insomnia, and many sinking turns during the night, in one of which, they seem to think, or rather hope, that I may pass away, although I do not believe that my time has come yet, and trust that I may be spared to engage in the Lord's service for some years to come. At times they seem to act more like incarnate fiends than rational beings, and all because they want to get the amount of my $2,000 policy, and to secure to the daughter at once the house we live in, on which she has a small mortgage, and in which there should be an equity of $2,000 more. This I know from their own lips. Scarcely a day is allowed to pass without some fresh annoyance, and I believe they are trying to make their relatives believe that my temper is so bad that my wife cannot live with me alone, which is absolutely untrue. Covetousness is the root of the whole trouble.

In their present state of feeling there is no telling what might happen. And I write this note to request that in case of my death whilst there is a policy of insurance upon my life, I would like you to cause a thorough and searching enquiry to be made into the cause of my death. Other things than I have stated seem to make this course desirable.

In the event of my death, I would like my body to be laid in Hamilton Cemetery, between the remains of my first and second wives, where a space has been reserved for it.

Your affectionate uncle,
W. J. FENTON.

P.S.—The sort of thing referred to herein has been kept up pretty constantly ever since Mr. and Mrs. S. with their family came to live in the house with us, and mother and daughter are pretty generally regarded as bright amiable women. I never would have believed it possible that they could treat me as they do. W. J. F.

For years together I have never known my wife to kneel alone in private prayer, or to read the Scriptures alone, and when I asked how she could live in that kind of way, she would answer that she always said her prayers in bed. And yet, although I had lost all confidence in any professions she had ever made, and was convinced that she had long been leading a double life, I can truly say that my daily prayer had been that I might be enabled to discharge my duty towards her, no matter how she acted towards me. It was only in the summer before our separation that I took her away with me on a business trip that lasted for several weeks, and she at length appeared to be quite broken down by the kindness which I showed towards her, and asked me if I could forgive her for the way she had acted. I told her then that I could forgive her freely, but that I could never forget the way in which I had heard her speak about me behind my back when she did not know that I was listening to her words, and that it must take time to establish confidence. For a short time after our return she seemed really anxious to make home what it should be, but soon relapsed into her old ways again, and several circumstances caused such grave misgivings as to her conduct that my old heart trouble returned, and when she persisted in getting a separation and separate maintenance, I was thankful to be relieved of her presence at almost any cost, although quite satisfied that she had no moral claim upon me to be supported in idleness, even if I were wealthy, which she knows is not the case.

When the paragraph referred to was first read by me, I saw at once that if it had in your mind any reference to me, you had been imposed upon by some false statements, which, as a Christian man, you should never have acted upon without first hearing what I had to say on the subject. My first act after reading it was to get on my knees before God, and ask Him to "search me, and try me, and see if there was any evil way in me, and lead me in the way everlasting." I know how easy it is for Christians sometimes to make mistakes, and imagine that they are acting for the glory of God, when they are only trying to gain some selfish ends, and for a short time feared that I might have been pursuing a mistaken course. But, after reviewing the whole matter in His presence, I was fully convinced that it was honorable labor in a legitimate business in which I was engaged, and that my motive is to act honestly, and glorify God with the proceeds of my labor, and I rose from my knees with the peace of God in my heart, and praised Him for His unchanging love and faithfulness.

I defy any man to charge me in an open, straightforward manner with dishonorable conduct as a business man in a single instance during the whole course of my business life for the past fifty years. But for fifteen or sixteen years past slanders have been whispered against me by Brethren excluded from our meetings for their misconduct, who presumed upon my forbearance, but dared not openly make any charge against me. Knowing this, I had frankly invited you to ask me for explanations in event of your having heard anything to my discredit. I have been honored as the recipient of abusive anonymous letters from Brethren, and so-called Holiness People, who boast of their own sinlessness, and in one instance some leaders of a meeting of Brethren in this city wrote a defamatory letter about me to another meeting, which they would not allow me to see, and the main ground of complaint in which I believe was the publication of my book on "The Unity of the Spirit."

That a few persons of extreme views in both these

classes should be annoyed at the publication of this book is not to be wondered at, but I had always given you credit personally for holding and teaching sound doctrine yourself on the subject of Holiness, although I would have preferred to see you take a more decided stand in correcting the extravagances of others in the Alliance meetings. This would have made the work of those who, like myself, were trying to conduct such meetings on a Scriptural basis, much easier, and I think that I wrote you to this effect before the last Alliance Convention for which I arranged in Toronto. I could not conscientiously remain connected with any work, and take part in the meetings where error was introduced, without protesting against it, and thus it happened, that when Mr. Dowie's Association, with Dr. Zimmerman and Mr. Salmon at its head, was established, and nearly all the Alliance people drawn in with them, I gave up the unequal struggle, and withdrew from the Alliance, as I have already stated. That this action should cause you to entertain any bitter feelings towards me I never imagined possible. And, although I wrote you afterwards to let me know if there was anything else you had against me, you have never replied. But now my wife is in fellowship in Mr. Salmon's Bethany meeting, her slanders are accepted as truth, Mrs. Salmon talks about her having had such a hard time of it whilst living with me, and immediately after leaving their society in this city you wrote that paragraph, which, it seems to me, you must have known would be regarded as applicable to me.

I have no reason to suppose that you have any other cause to be offended with me than my withdrawal from your work in this city, and my speaking and writing plainly to yourself and others in reference to the unscriptural theories, and extravagant testimonies of some of the so-called "Holiness People," some of whom actually declared that after receiving the Holy Spirit they did not any longer need the Word of God. Is it possible that you could have imagined that by striking such a cruel blow as that in your paragraph, the husband who had suffered in silence for so many years could be punished for having left the Alliance over ten years ago, and that at the same time a left-handed certificate of character might be given to the woman, now returned to the Alliance, who has by her misconduct proved herself to be unworthy of the name of "wife"?

That you should stoop so low as to listen to vile slanders against one whom you knew to have been engaged for many years in a humble way in Gospel service, and who had loyally tried to serve you to the best of his ability, so long as this could be done with fidelity to the truth of Scripture, and that you should, in the Alliance paper try to inflict pain or injury upon such a one, by imputing the worst of motives to his honest labor in a legitimate and necessary business, is something of which I should never have thought it possible that you could be guilty.

The Word of God commands me to "owe to no man "anything save love," and I therefore believe it to be my duty as an honest Christian business man, to use all legitimate means to obtain freedom from every liability to others. It would not be right for me to contribute to the Lord's work large sums of money belonging not to me, but to those who had just claims against me. This is precisely the ground that was taken by D. L. Moody, when asking contributions to his work at his meetings in Toronto, when he distinctly stated that he did not want those who were in debt to contribute. And, in this connection, as I have already written to you so plainly about my own financial affairs, I trust you will excuse me for saying that I do not believe the methods you take in raising money for missions are as glorifying to God as those of George Muller, J. Hudson Taylor, George S. Fisher, and many others, who take up no collections, but simply make known the needs of the various mission fields, and call for the workers, and then ask the Lord for the money to carry on the work, and, trusting in Him, they find that he is a faithful covenant-keeping God, who has never failed those who fully trust Him, although their faith may be sorely tried.

I cannot see that it is right to ask people who are in debt to promise payment, within a certain time, of money for the Lord's work, in the mission fields or otherwise, to impress upon their minds that what they have thus promised is a debt due to the Lord, and not to the persons who have obtained their promises, and then to impress upon their minds still further by means of the Alliance paper, that their missionary debt has the first claim, although God has distinctly commanded them to " owe no man anything."

It appears to me, therefore, that the last paragraph on the same page as that about which this letter is written, is not likely, if its teaching is followed to promote honest dealing with our fellow-men, and on this account I cannot endorse it. This paragraph is headed, "How to Give to Missions," and begins as follows:—

"Put down your Missionary Debt as the first "claim. When you pay your weekly bills, do not "say, 'I must pay my debts first, and if there is "anything left I will give it,' but put God's claim at "the head of the list, and then all the others will be "more easily paid, for you are a debtor to Him and "to a lost world much more than to your butcher or "baker," etc., etc. Does this language indicate that the writer of it is looking for supplies to the living God alone, " whose are the gold and silver, and the " cattle upon a thousand hills " ? Or does it betray a fear lest some debtors, who in the enthusiasm of a large meeting, had promised to pay more than they could afford, might feel conscientiously bound to pay their creditors before fulfilling promises which they should never have made ? It is easy to " strain at a "gnat and swallow a camel." To endeavor to cast blame upon others for doing something which is perfectly right and lawful, and undertaken with the best of motives, and at the same time for the fault-finder to do, or advise others to do, that which may lead to acts of downright dishonesty.

At the same time I can understand, from my own experience, how a Christian may feel himself justified in contributing a fair proportion of his earnings " as the Lord has prospered " to Christian work and worship, and at the same time be doing his best to get out of debt to his fellow-men.

Whilst I differ from you on this subject, however, I do not judge your motives, and will try to put the best construction on what you do. And I sincerely trust that in the future you will act in the same spirit towards me, and any other person who may be similarly situated.

I do not for a moment justify my purchasing all those lands over 30 years ago as a speculation, nor do I justify my purchase of a large amount of property in this city ten or twelve years ago, which was subject to mortgages, that kept me always in doubt about what I could conscientiously contribute to the Lord's work. On the contrary, I have often warned others by my experience not to involve themselves in debt at all. I have also confessed as sin my disobedience to the command not to owe anything to anyone, and the sin has been forgiven, but the liabilities to my fellowmen remain, and it is with a view to getting these removed that I have been working day and night for the past two years, and not "to get rich quick," although if it please God to spare my life a little longer and so prosper this business, that I may not only be able to get out of debt, but also to earn a large amount of money to spend in His service, I shall be sincerely thankful.

I can say with truth that in the promotion of this Company, from first to last, I have asked God to guide and enable me to use for His glory any means that may be earned thereby, and He has wonderfully guided through what often seemed insurmountable obstacles, thus far, and I trust will continue to guide and bless in the future. But if, after having honestly done my best, He should see fit to withhold His blessing, and honest poverty await me, I trust that I may be enabled with cheerful submission to say, "Thy will be done," just as readily as you would probably say these words, if He withholds the money required for your work in the mission field, notwithstanding all your efforts to obtain it, by such means as you have seen fit to use.

In writing this letter to you, I have used plain language, that cannot well be misunderstood, because of the cowardly attacks made upon me from time to time within the past fifteen or sixteen years, by parties who dare not openly make any charge against me. My character, as a consistent Christian business man, is dearer to me than all the wealth of all the world. I have nearly reached the allotted span of human life, and it has been impressed upon me for some time past that slander, from any quarter, should no longer be submitted to in silence, more especially after the wicked threats made use of by my wife and her daughter, as to what they would say if they did not succeed in their avaricious designs. I regard the paragraph written by you, just after leaving Toronto, where my wife has been attending your meetings (and is on intimate terms with Mr. Salmon, who presided at them, and with his wife), as the first public manifestation that their threats are being carried out. They had boasted that if I denied any of their assertions, there would be the word, and if necessary, the oaths, of three against one, but after they learned that I had been for some time keeping a diary, in which their conduct and language were recorded, they were evidently alarmed at the possible consequences of their behaviour, which was considerably modified for the following year, until the daughter, son-in-law, and three grandchildren, removed from our house to another place of residence, after living in part of the same house with us for over two years. For the sake of the grandchildren, to whom I have always been attached, and with whom I am still on friendly terms, I would have continued to keep silence regarding the past conduct of their mother and grandmother, and for their sakes I did not intend that my diary should be published, but only that a number of typewritten copies of it should be left in the hands of some personal friends, as an ante-mortem statement, to be used as a means of refuting any slanders that might be circulated after my death. But your apparent eagerness to cause an impression that I am engaged in some discreditable business, has compelled me to make known the circumstances in which I have been placed.

Self-vindication is at no time a pleasant task, but as you have found in your own experience, it is sometimes unavoidable, and, after slander has been endured in silence for many years, there is a proper limit to the forbearance that should be exercised, because continued silence might only be regarded as the tacit admission of conscious guilt.

I shall, therefore, consider myself at liberty to defend my character against the imputation of dishonorable motives contained in your paragraph, and against the statements of my wife and her daughter which, I believe, led, directly or indirectly, to your writing as you did, although it is quite likely that you did not converse with either of them. And in making my defence I shall endeavor to give it as wide publicity as the false imputations which your paper contained against me.

Yours very truly,
W. J. Fenton.

P.S.—I send you herewith a copy of the last issue of Dominion Fence Company's Manual, by which you will see the nature of the business that I am "promoting."

In justice to Rev. A. B. Simpson, President of the Christian and Missionary Alliance, New York, I herewith send to each person to whom a copy of my open letter to him of March 15th, 1902, was sent, a copy of the following correspondence between us that has since taken place.

W. J. FENTON.

NEW YORK, March 25, 1902.

DEAR BRO. FENTON:—Miss L—— has handed me an open letter of yours to me, to-day. I wish you had asked me about this before publishing it. It is an unfortunate mistake. I had not the slightest reference to you when I put the editorial referred to in our paper, and had never heard a word of your family or business troubles till to-day. I did not even know that you had been engaged in any speculative business. I have always had the kindest and most friendly regards towards you, and remembered with love the fellowship of former days. I was not conscious of meeting you in Toronto in any but the most friendly spirit.

The point I made in my editorial was with respect to some foolish speculations here that have involved many good people in danger. And if you will read an editorial in this week's Alliance you will see that we have had to remove one of our own Trustees for dealing recklessly in these things.

I regret that my long absences from home and overwhelming pressure of work, have rendered it simply impossible to write to you as I would so gladly have done.

With the kindest Christian regards and deep regret for your domestic and business trials.

I am, my dear Brother,
Your Friend in Him,
A. B. SIMPSON.

TORONTO, March 29, 1902.

REV. A. B. SIMPSON, Nyack, New York.

DEAR BRO. SIMPSON.—Your letter of 25th inst. has been received, and I can assure you that it gave me great pain to have to publish and circulate to a limited extent my deference to your editorial, which I could not help regarding under all the circumstances as a personal attack, if you were aware when writing it, that I was engaged in promoting any business. I regret to say that I cannot accept as correct the following statement in your letter:—" I have always had the kindest and most friendly regard towards you, and remembered with love the fellowship of former days. I was not conscious of meeting you in Toronto in any but the most friendly spirit." The reason for my non-acceptance of this statement is that on the occasion of my meeting and greeting you cordially, at a convention, after my withdrawal from the Alliance, you not only treated me coldly, but in such an unfriendly manner, that I wrote you in the most friendly spirit to find out the reason, and never received any reply. But I will take it for granted that you must have forgotten the circumstances.

I did not write my open letter to elicit your sympathy for my own sufferings by reason of my wife's conduct, or through losses by depreciation of real estate values in this city; but only to show you the gross injustice of your remarks with reference to the promotion of companies generally, and the strong presumption raised by the circumstances that a personal attack was intended by the writer of the editorial.

You have not denied being aware, when the editorial was written, that I was acting as the "promoter" of a business of some kind, and it was the use of this word that would identify me in the minds of some of the readers of your paper. Nor have you denied knowing at the same time of the separation from my wife, who is now in your meeting here. While your letter is couched in the most friendly and brotherly terms, the issue raised by your editorial and my reply appears to be thus evaded.

If you had not heard before your editorial was written that I was promoting a business, and was separated from my wife, I am bound as a Christian man to accept your declaration to that effect, and will do so with pleasure. But at the same time I must be perfectly candid with you and say that without such a declaration, and looking all the facts squarely in the face, it seemed impossible to avoid any other conclusions than those in my open letter.

What I felt most keenly from one whom I had esteemed so highly, was the imputation without knowledge of the facts, of wrong motives in promoting a necessary manufacturing business. I regarded this as being contrary to the teaching of 1 Cor. xiii., and if, in this I have done you injustice, and been betrayed into anything that might appear like a spirit of retaliation, I am sorry for it, and hope to be forgiven, and I sincerely trust that the Lord's work in which you are engaged may not be in any way injured thereby.

Nothing will give me greater pleasure than to have every barrier to perfect fellowship removed, and I most earnestly desire and pray that what has occurred, although painful, may only be productive of lasting good to all concerned.

Yours in the Lord,
W. J. FENTON.

NEW YORK, April 2, 1902.

MY DEAR BROTHER FENTON:—Your letter of March 29 is received, and I hasten to assure you that I was not aware when I wrote my editorial referred to that you and your wife had had any trouble of any kind. I was not aware that you were promoting the sale of stock of any kind, and I had not the remotest reference to you in that paper.

I have no objections to the sale of stock in any honest company. I had reference, however, to a class of speculations becoming very common in this country, in which poor people are advised by men having some religious influence to buy stocks under the assurance that they will increase in value five or ten fold when there are no facts to justify these promises.

Some of our own Alliance people have unfortunately been drawn into these nets, and it was because they had written to us for information that we felt bound to give this note of warning.

Yours sincerely in Him,
A. B. SIMPSON.

P.S.—The interview and letter you refer to I have not the slightest recollection of. I don't even know if I ever received the letter, or I would have answered it.

TORONTO, April 5th, 1902.
REV. A. B. SIMPSON, 692 Eighth Ave, New York.

MY DEAR BROTHER SIMPSON:—I have received your letter of 2nd inst., and gladly accept your declaration that when the editorial was written you were not aware that I was promoting a company, and was separated from my wife. This as a matter of course relieves you from the suspicion of having intentionally made a personal attack upon me, which the remarkable combination of circumstances seemed to indicate. But although you did not intend to do me any injury, the effect of your editorial upon the minds of others who know me, and read your paper, was just the same as if you had been aware of the above facts. And the publication seven weeks afterwards of the paragraph regarding Dr. Furry, would not be likely to lessen the injury done, if I had not sent you my open letter, which made known the circumstances in which I had been placed, and the motives that led me to work at the legitimate and necessary business in which I am engaged.

This incident shows how careful public journalists need to be in commenting upon matters affecting the public welfare that they do not understand. It was most unreasonable to condemn, in scathing terms, the "promoters" of all companies, because some parties thus engaged had acted dishonestly. You might just as well denounce the whole medical profession as criminals, because some doctors had been found guilty of malpractice; or the whole legal profession as rogues, because some lawyers are only pettifogging tricksters.

I am very thankful, however, for your assurance that there was no intention to make a personal allusion to me in your editorial, and in justice to you I will send a copy of our correspondence to each person to whom a copy of my open letter was addressed.

Yours sincerely in Christ,
W. J. FENTON.

CPSIA information can be obtained
at www.ICGtesting.com
Printed in the USA
LVHW022216170323
741893LV00032B/1420